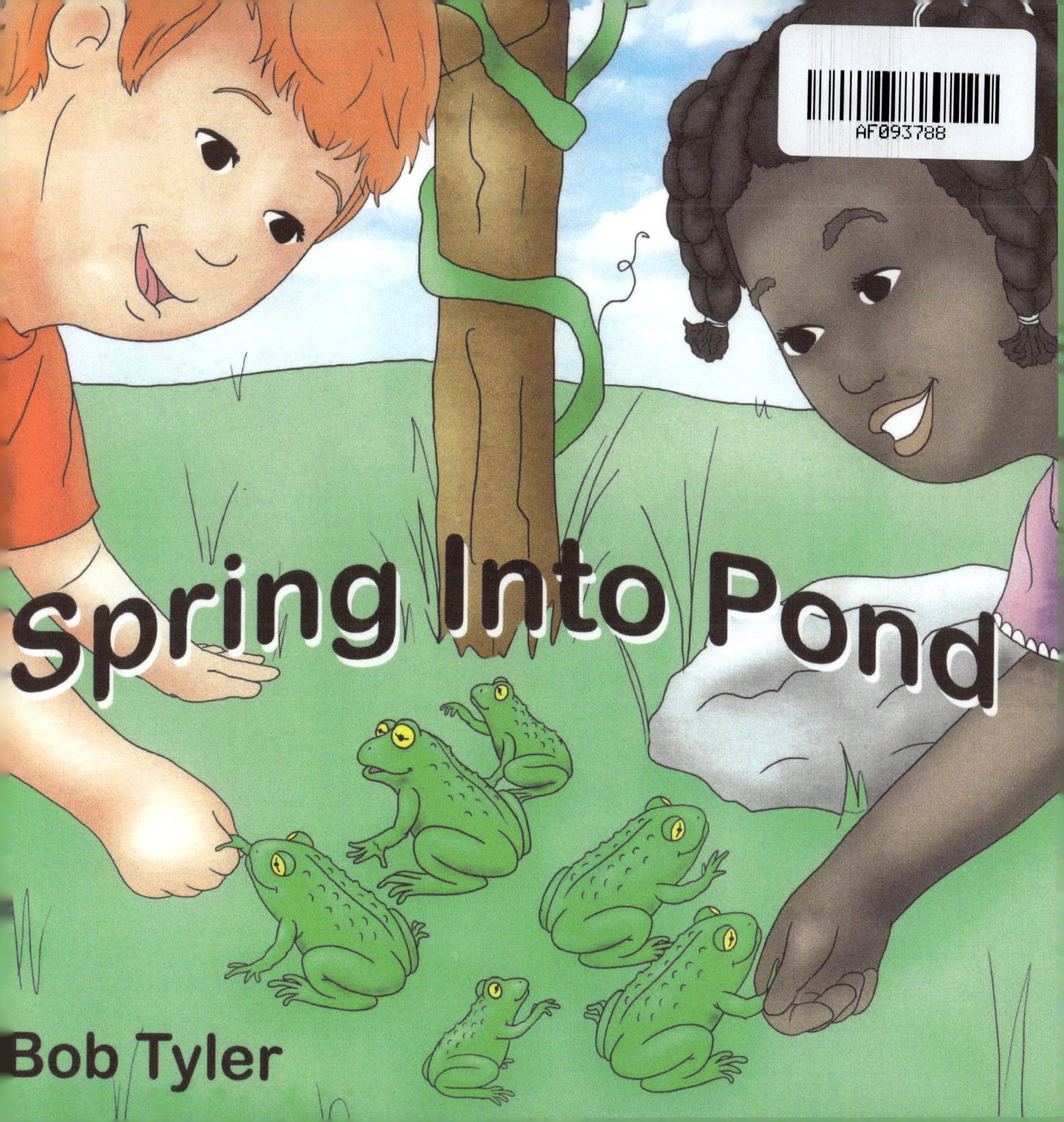

Copyright © 2025 Bob Tyler.

All rights reserved. No part of this book may be reproduced, stored, or transmitted by any means—whether auditory, graphic, mechanical, or electronic—without written permission of both publisher and author, except in the case of brief excerpts used in critical articles and reviews. Unauthorized reproduction of any part of this work is illegal and is punishable by law.

ISBN: 979-8-89419-729-6 (sc)
ISBN: 979-8-89419-462-2 (hc)
ISBN: 979-8-89419-463-9 (e)

Because of the dynamic nature of the Internet, any web addresses or links contained in this book may have changed since publication and may no longer be valid. The views expressed in this work are solely those of the author and do not necessarily reflect the views of the publisher, and the publisher hereby disclaims any responsibility for them.

One Galleria Blvd., Suite 1900, Metairie, LA 70001
(504) 702-6708

Dedicated to Deb and Siddhi

Many thanks to Hans and Barb Feldmann,
Sandi Lewis, and Doris Heginbothom
for their creative suggestions and to
the Authorhouse team for its invaluable
graphic and editorial contributions.

 Bruster

 Alicia

 Alexander

Hoppie, what are you doing in our pitcher of lemonade?

It is very impolite to stereotype anyone with a pet name. Actually, my name is Alexander Pole.

Okay Alexander Pole, what are you doing in our pitcher of lemonade?

Well, I was hopping around on your picnic table and temptation overcame me.

But you're a frog, not an ice cube, and I think it is very impolite of you to place yourself in our beverage.

I apologize. But it is soooo refreshing.

Now I suppose you expect us to provide a straw so that it's easier for you to have a sip.

No need for sarcasm. Anyway, I don't need a straw. I absorb liquids through my skin.

Well then perhaps you'd prefer to have found a bowl of a more suitable liquid on the table in which you could have immersed yourself and enhanced your dining pleasure.

I know that you're still being sarcastic, but actually, I'd prefer a bowl of gazpacho.

What is gazpacho?

It's a very tasty cold soup that is made with cucumbers, tomatoes, peppers, and onions.

I'm sorry, but my culinary skills are quite limited.

In that case, perhaps you could consider building a pond for me and covering it with tons of water lilies.

You can't be serious.

I can dream, can't I?

Alicia, what do you think? I know that I couldn't begin to build a pond without your help and advice.

Well..., Alexander does seem like a nice frog. I think it would be fun to build a pond for him. Let's do it!

Oh, you make me uncontrollably happy! Ribbit! Ribbit! Ribbit!

Get a grip, Alexander.

Alexander, if we do build a pond for you, will you live there all by yourself?

As a matter of fact, no. I'd be moving in with my wife and our son, Tad.

Anyone else?

Why yes. The Wogg family. The Woggs are our closest friends.

Are they the frogs sitting over there under the grape vine?

Yes. Let me introduce you.

Okay.

This is Mrs. Pole and our son, Tad, and this is Mr. and Mrs. Wogg and their daughter, Polly.

Very pleased to make your acquaintance. My name is Bruster McToosel and this is my friend and neighbor, Alicia Peppertree.

It's very nice to meet you all.

And we are all very pleased to meet you. Although my family and friends have not yet learned to speak your language, they do understand much of what you are saying.

How in the world did you ever learn to understand and speak English?

That is a very long story. Let's save it for another time.

Oh...Okay.

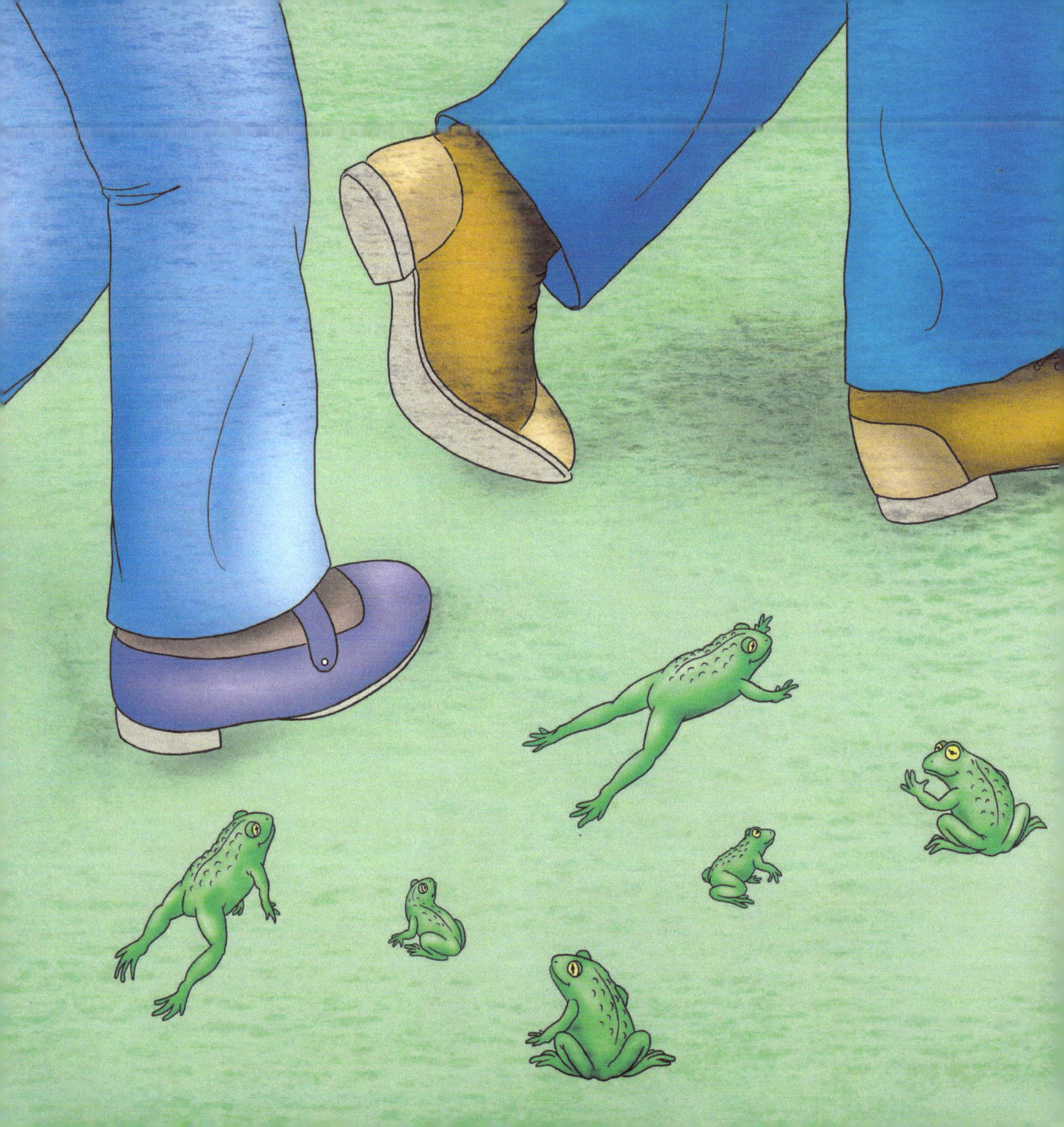

Follow me. I know the perfect place to build our pond.

Alicia really knows how to get things done.

I can see that.

This is a nice location, Alicia, but this spring with its run-off stream in the middle of your back yard seems way too small for a pond.

You're right. But notice that this spring is about two feet deep, just the right depth for our pond. In fact, this is an artesian spring, which means that underground water is forced up into it by underground pressure. We'll start by staking out a big circle around the spring to show us where we want the edge of the pond to be.

Then we'll dig out the ground from within the circle to the same depth as the spring. Right?

That makes a lot of sense. Then the water from the spring will fill up the space that we have dug out and make a nice pond for us.

You are one smart frog, Alexander.

Why thank you, Bruster.

What tools and materials are we going to need?

First we'll need a hammer, several wooden stakes to mark out the edge of our pond, a thin pole, a piece of string four feet long, a pipe to be used for drainage, two shovels, and a garden rake.

I'm sure that we can find all of those items in my dad's workshop in the basement. I'll be right back.

I'll run home and let my mom know what we're planning to see if it's okay with her.

Now, we have all the materials we need to get started. So let's begin by marking out the edge of our circle.

How will we do that?

First pound the thin pole in the center of the spring.

Then what?

You can then tie a small loop in one end of our string and slip the loop over the pole.

Go on.

I get it! Then you can tie the other end around me and I'll stretch the string straight out to its full four-foot length and keep it tight while I hop around the pole

That means that you'll be hopping around the spring in a circle with a four-foot radius.

Bruster, you should really explain that the radius of a circle is the distance from the center of the circle to the edge of the circle itself.

And isn't the distance all the way around a circle called its circumference?

You amaze me, Alexander! How in the world did you know that?

I'm a frog, not a rock.

The circumference of the circle is the distance you will have hopped when you get all the way around and I pound in the last stake. In fact, the entire outside edge of the circle, rather than its length, is often referred to as the "circumference" of the circle.

Ribbit! Ribbit! Ribbit! I can hardly wait to get all the way around the circumference.

I think that we work very well together.

Just pound a stake into the ground at each point where I land after taking a hop.

These stakes will mark out the edge of our pond. Right?

Correct!!!

I guess it's time for Alicia and me to start digging.

Yes. We should start digging from the edge of the circle and work our way in toward the spring. We can dig down and remove about two feet of ground from within the circle until we get to the spring itself.

Let's throw each shovelful out on the boundary marked by the stakes. Then we'll have a nice bank around our pond.

I'll start by positioning the drainage pipe so that it connects our pond to the old run-off stream bed after we finish making the bank.

Great idea!!! Then the pond will always have fresh spring water coming in and will not overflow the bank.

You know, this pond is filling up with water and starting to look very nice.

My mom said that she would go to the nursery and pick up some grass seed, a bale of straw, and some water lilies. I'll see if she's come back. See you in a minute.

While you're gone, we'll smooth out the bank with the rake and get it ready for planting the grass seed.

Great idea!!!

Now let's spread the grass seed on the bank around the edge of our pond and cover it with straw. This straw will help the grass to grow by keeping it moist and by preventing birds from eating the seeds.

I'll dig some holes in the bottom of the pond and plant the lilies.

Bruster and Alicia, we're really going to like living here.

It will be great to have you as our new neighbors.

Wow! This is really beautiful. Thank you Bruster and Alicia. Ribbit! Ribbit! Ribbit! Ribbit! Ribbit! Ribbit!

About the Author

Bob Tyler received his PhD in Mathematics from Syracuse University in 1971 and taught mathematics at Susquehanna University in Selinsgrove, Pennsylvania until his retirement in 2002, when he received the Susquehanna Award for Distinguished Teaching. Since retirement he has written a country song, a dialog explaining the meaning of different orders of infinity, and this book. He is currently working on a second country song. His interest in writing children's stories comes from the many hours of enjoyment he had in creating bedtime stories for and with his own children.

www.ingramcontent.com/pod-product-compliance
Lightning Source LLC
LaVergne TN
LVHW070442070526
838199LV00036B/683